THE

Holy Spirit

WITH YOU,
IN YOU, &
UPON YOU

By Sheila Kay

The Holy Spirit With You, In You, & Upon You, Paperback

ISBN: 978-1-951280-35-2

Cover Design: Don Patton, Image Credit: Freepik

Dedication

I dedicate this book to all who love the wonderful Triune God that we serve. Who long to go deeper with Him from glory to glory to glory. To those who hunger and thirst for more of Him and can't ever seem to get filled. For those who have walked out into the deep, whose only conversation is about God, His Word, His love for us, and longing to spend eternity with Him. For, we are all like- minded, and of one accord, and we are to be the Bride of Christ forever. I love you all, Elisha

Contents

Introduction

John 16:8-11 - 8 And when he is come, he will reprove the world of sin, and of righteousness, and of judgment: 9 Of sin, because they believe not on me; 10 Of righteousness, because I go to my Father, and ye see me no more; 11 Of judgment, because the prince of this world is judged.

I am in hope that the title and the contents of this book and its topic is as exciting for you to read as it has been for me to write. It is important that we continue to remember and grow in the things we have learned pertaining to the Bible throughout our lives, and our slow growth with God over the years of walking with Him.

One of the most memorable comments from the Bible, that I often think about is "We are in this world, but not of it."[1] All that we do requires faith, much faith… and more FAITH.

The Godhead, the marvelous three in one of Father God, Son, and Holy Spirit, have all had their share in fulfilling their assignments and roles in this

[1] See John 15:19, 17:14-16

magnificent formation of our Spirit, soul, and body. They played an active part in the writing of the Holy Bible and the creation of the world, and still play an active role in authoring our salvation, working our sanctification, and showing us how to be Holy, as He is holy.

We also play an important role in the formation and timeline of how the Spirit works, as he moves from glory to glory in our lives. The timeline is different for each of us. Some children are raised in church and are filled with the Spirit at an early age because of exposure to the things of God at home, through family, and at Church. While others of us have been led down a sinful path and have had to face numerous obstacles that we have had to overcome before we can even begin to learn the basics.

And the basics is where we will begin.

The Holy Spirit. Who is He, what is He, where is He, what does He do, how does He work in your life? The subject is vast, and the Bible contains wonderful little nuggets that we may feast on. Here is a list of some of His attributes:

HOLY SPIRIT'S NAMES	THE SPIRITS OF GOD
The Holy Ghost	The Spirit of Holiness
The third person of the Godhead	The Spirit of God's Son
Abiding Presence	The Spirit of Glory
Christ in the Believer	The Spirit of Christ
The Comforter	The Spirit of Adoption
The Eternal Spirit	The Spirit of Life
The Law of the Spirit	The Spirit of Truth
The Living Water	The Spirit of Prophecy
The Promise of the Father	The Spirit of the Father
The Unction	

In this book, I will explain who the Holy Spirit is and how we must surrender to the Lord before moving on to greater revelations and power. Also, I will share how my life changed forever after the Holy Spirit was with me, in me, and when He came upon me for service in God's Kingdom. I hope you will be blessed by this book and that it will inspire you to go deeper into the depths of God. My prayer is that you will gain understanding of how to live by the power of the Holy Spirit in your own life. This wonderful treasure gift that God has given us! Glory!

How Does the Holy Spirit Work?

The Holy Spirit works through the Mighty Three in One:

> *John 5:26 - 26 For as the Father hath life in himself; so hath he given to the Son to have life in himself;*

This Scripture tells us that the Father is the ultimate source of life. He has life in Himself that He has given to the Son. The Father is the source, the Son is the channel of that source, and the Holy Spirit is the power that flows through that channel. The Mighty Three in One in action. Glory!

Before God speaks, the Spirit always moves. The Spirit releases the source and touches our life. It is Jesus, the Son who poured out the Holy Spirit from the Father.

> *Acts 1:8a - 8 But ye shall receive power, after that the Holy Ghost is come upon you...*

> *Acts 2:33 - 33 Therefore being by the right*

hand of God exalted, and having received of the Father the promise of the Holy Ghost, he hath shed forth this, which ye now see and hear.

There are different emblems of the Holy Spirit throughout the Bible that represent the Holy Spirit to us.

The Dove:

John 1:32-33 - 32 And John bare record, saying, I saw the Spirit descending from heaven like a dove, and it abode upon him. 33 And I knew him not: but he that sent me to baptize with water, the same said unto me, Upon whom thou shalt see the Spirit descending, and remaining on him, the same is he which baptizes with the Holy Ghost.

Oil/Anointing:

Luke 4:18 - 18 The Spirit of the Lord [is] upon me, because he hath anointed me to preach the gospel to the poor; he hath sent me to heal the brokenhearted, to preach deliverance to the captives, and recovering of sight to the blind, to set at liberty them that are bruised,

Acts 10:38 - 38 How God anointed Jesus of Nazareth with the Holy Ghost and with power: who went about doing good, and healing all that were oppressed of the devil; for God was with him.

Hebrews 1:9 - 9 Thou hast loved righteousness, and hated iniquity; therefore God, [even] thy God, hath anointed thee with the oil of gladness above thy fellows.

Water:

John 7:37-39 - 37 In the last day, that great [day] of the feast, Jesus stood and cried, saying, If any man thirst, let him come unto me, and drink. 38 He that believeth on me, as the scripture hath said, out of his belly shall flow rivers of living water. 39 (But this spake he of the Spirit, which they that believe on him should receive: for the Holy Ghost was not yet [given]; because that Jesus was not yet glorified.)

Isaiah 44:3 - 3 For I will pour water upon him that is thirsty, and floods upon the dry ground: I will pour my spirit upon thy seed, and my blessing upon thine offspring:

A Seal:

Ephesians 1:13 - 13 In whom ye also [trusted], after that ye heard the word of truth, the gospel of your salvation: in whom also after that ye believed, ye were sealed with that holy Spirit of promise,

Ephesians 4:30 - 30 And grieve not the holy Spirit of God, whereby ye are sealed unto the day of redemption.

2 Corinthians 1:22 - 22 Who hath also sealed us, and given the earnest of the Spirit in our hearts.

Wind:

John 3:8 - 8 The wind bloweth where it listeth, and thou hearest the sound thereof, but canst not tell whence it cometh, and whither it goeth: so is every one that is born of the Spirit.

Acts 2:1-2 - 1 And when the day of Pentecost was fully come, they were all with one accord in one place. 2 And suddenly there came a sound from heaven as of a rushing mighty wind, and it filled all the house where they were sitting.

Fire:

> *Exodus 3:2 - 2 And the angel of the LORD appeared unto him in a flame of fire out of the midst of a bush: and he looked, and, behold, the bush burned with fire, and the bush [was] not consumed.*

> *Leviticus 9:23b-24 – 23b ...and the glory of the LORD appeared unto all the people. 24 And there came a fire out from before the LORD, and consumed upon the altar the burnt offering and the fat: [which] when all the people saw, they shouted, and fell on their faces.*

We receive the Holy Spirit in us when we first believe that Jesus is Lord.[2] We receive it by faith and not by works, nor by our own obedience to the Law[3]. We receive it by repentance, being born again, by obeying God, and through the baptism of the Holy Ghost.[4]

The Holy Spirit is the sustaining power of the believer, proving that Christ abides within a person, proving that one is truly saved and is indeed, the

---

[2] See Ephesians 1:13

[3] See Galatians 3:2

[4] See Acts 2:32; John 3:5; Acts 1:4-5; 1 Corinthians 2:12-13

Temple of The Holy Spirit.[5]

The infilling of the Holy Spirit follows our obedience to God and His discipline for our lives, including walking in the commands and teachings of Jesus with a blameless heart.[6] The Holy Spirit also indwells the church in a special way, for we are the church, the Temple of God. And if anyone defiles this temple God will destroy him, for we are holy.[7]

There are many different Church denominations and many published Bibles that attest to their beliefs. However, they all say the Holy Spirit is with you, and with all of us to prepare us for salvation. God is omnipresent by His Spirit and gives mankind a conscience of truth vs error and right vs wrong.[8] But the Holy Spirit does not yet dwell in you until you believe that Jesus is Lord.

The Holy Spirit comes to dwell in you when you believe. And as you continue to grow in faith, you are led to a Pentecostal moment when the Holy Spirit through a mighty rushing wind enters you causing you to be baptized in the Holy Ghost and Fire. Glory! As we continue to grow in the wonders of the Spirit,

---

[5] See 1 John 3:24, 4:12-13; 1 Corinthians 6:19-20

[6] See John 14:21-26

[7] See 1 Corinthians 3:16-17

[8] See Romans 2:14

our faith grows, by leaps and bounds from 20%, to 60%, to 100%. Going deeper and deeper out into the deep. Going from your ankles to your knees to your shoulders in the river of God, until you are swimming in His Glory!

The Glorious Holy Spirit is with us, in us and upon us for service in God's Kingdom. This service is directed by the Holy Spirit and the action begins through you. As you step out in faith, your obedience flips the switch to the Spirit. Because of your obedience and proper use of the anointing, your hunger for more of God will continue to grow and grow and grow. We go deeper as we long to draw closer to the Lord. We are in Him and He in us. We are the Temple of God.

Section One:

The Holy Spirit With You

The Holy Spirit With You

The Holy Spirit is all-powerful (omnipotent.) He is also ever-present, He is everywhere, (omnipresent.) However, prior to the cross at Calvary, the Holy Spirit was limited and could not dwell within a person. But when Jesus ascended to the right hand of the Father as our intercessor, and when the Day of Pentecost had fully come, The Holy Spirit stepped into His role to fulfill the mission God had called Him to do on earth.

The Holy Spirit is with us to open our hearts to accept Christ. He is with us as a wee small inner voice, preparing the way for us to the Lord. He is with us when we accept and receive the new birth, He is with us as we invite the Lord into our hearts, and at that moment our sins are totally forgiven, covered by the blood of Jesus Christ. When the Father sees us, He sees the blood of Jesus rather than our sins.

> *Romans 3:11 - 11 There is none that understandeth, there is none that seeketh after God.*

This says that there is no one who seeks God. This

means that it is God, through the Holy Spirit, who seeks after us. The Holy Spirit comes after us, He pursues us, chooses us, and directs our steps, preparing us for salvation through faith in Jesus.

Why did Jesus come into the earth? "I came not to call the righteous, but sinners to repentance."[9] Repentance is necessary to enter the kingdom of God. What kingdom are you going to follow? The Kingdom of Satan or the Kingdom of God.

Repentance is an inward decision or change of mind resulting in our outward actions of turning from sin. It is the power of God the Holy Spirit with us that actually brings the change in our mind and heart, in spite of our life as a sinner. We are told that "unless we turn, we will perish."[10] Repentance plus conversion results in justification.

Now, no man can say that Christ is Lord except by the Holy Spirit. It is the Holy Spirit alone, who reveals the Lordship of Christ to us.[11] He is with us to guide us, to teach us, to tell us, and show us, while leading our hearts toward salvation. Our salvation occurs through the cross and blood of Jesus, giving His life for our belief and faith in Him as our Savior,

---

[9] See Luke 5:32

[10] See Luke 13:3

[11] See 1 Corinthians 12:3

and the remission of our sins.

But now that Christ has ascended, the promise of the Holy Spirit has come as our comforter and our teacher. Just as Jesus prepared his disciples, we too will be taught by Him through the Spirit. The Holy Spirit is God's representative to mankind. For four thousand years the Holy Ghost moved through the earth seeking men worthy of being "moved upon" by Him. But now that the day of Pentecost has come, the Holy Spirit has been poured out for everyone who believes in Jesus.

When Jesus ministered on the earth, there were twelve apostles that identified with Jesus from the onset of His ministry. Of the twelve, there were three that stood out as being much closer than the others. They were intimately close to Jesus and perhaps near to His age, yet different from the others in ways, mannerism, education taste, temperament and understanding.

All of them were gathered with Jesus when He talked about the promise of the Holy Spirit.[12] All of the Apostles had the Holy Spirit *with them*, including Judas, but none of the Apostles had the Holy Spirit *in them* until the Day of Pentecost. The Day of Pentecost fell on Sunday morning after sunrise. They

[12] See John 14 & 16

gathered as Jesus had directed, praying and waiting for the promise of The Spirit.

> *Acts 1:2 - 2 Until the day in which he was taken up, after that he through the Holy Ghost had given commandments unto the apostles whom he had chosen:*

Christ did His works until He was taken up. After that, it was the Holy Spirit that was the speaker, the power, the agency, and the representative of God to people. For Jesus Christ was and now is, seated at the right hand of the Father Almighty, interceding for us.

The Holy Spirit could not come into the heart and life of the believer in the realm of baptism until Jesus died on the Cross, thereby taking the sins of man away.[13] Before the Holy Spirit dwelt ***with*** the believers, whereas now He dwells ***in*** them. The Holy Spirit can now come into the cleansed Temple and there He shall abide.

The abiding presence of the Holy Spirit is always there. He was with us from the beginning, He is in us when we believe and as we accept Christ as our Savior. He will never leave us nor forsake us, and He will be with us at the rapture and in heaven. He never,

[13] See 1 Peter 3:21

ever, leaves us.

This said, we will hunger and thirst for more of Him because He is that river of life that never shall run dry. He will feed our hunger and quench our thirst. A deeper hunger for God is planted in your heart. As you begin to hunger and thirst for more and more and more of Him, your innermost parts are being prepared, you are being formed and prepared, some, even purged of past sins.

My personal experience at this point of my hunger began early one afternoon. I entered my prayer closet and began to pray. Suddenly, a funnel-like whirlwind came through the window and entered my right eye. This pure white funnel with just a hint of emerald-green on the inner side of the funnel, continued to turn for twenty seconds and then the funnel moved into my left eye without missing a beat, for the same length of time as this mystical phenomenon continued.

That night as I slept, pieces of what appeared to be dark particles or specks, were thrown, or purged from both of my eyes. It was similar to a Star Wars movie, as the specks appeared to be cast out into space. I identified the purged particles as sin but did not want to identify them individually. I was just glad to be rid of the sin.

I was being prepared to receive the Holy Spirit. My body needed to be prepared through this cleansing and these stages of preparation. The Holy Spirit could not live in the filth of my sin.

But when the Holy Spirit came into me, I felt like a new person. Amazingly, I had no fear, for I knew it was of God. There was a calmness, a peaceful beauty to what had just taken place. It was as if I was being sanctified, set aside, being made pure to live for Him forever.

While the Holy Spirit is transitioning from being with us as He leads us to Jesus, to salvation, I consider this the growth period, the time the Spirit is moving in us. There are also different types of gifts that are given during our growth period. The gifts are only given to those who are born-again, who believe and are now beginning to follow Jesus Christ. As described earlier, the Father is the Source, the Son is the Channel of that Source, and the Holy Spirit is the Power that flows through that Channel and delivers the Gifts to us. As we grow in our knowledge and draw closer to the Lord, spiritual gifts are given so that other believers can benefit. (We'll talk about spiritual gifts in a later chapter.)

The fruit of the Spirit are given to show us how we are to walk and order our behavior. While the Holy

Spirit is in us, we receive the nine fruit of the Spirit: love, joy, peace, longsuffering, gentleness, goodness, faith, meekness, and temperance.[14] Living a Lifestyle in these basic fruits and growing in Holiness is part of the Source (the Father) being channeled to us and through us.

Without a doubt the place we want to enter and live, is in the Spirit. The place where God's presence is overwhelming, and the peace is indescribable.

Salvation is only the beginning, and only scratches the surface. The Holy Spirit will be with us as we grow in the Word of God. This growth is vitally important. We must grow from glory, to glory, to glory!

---

[14] See Galatians 5:22-25

Section Two:

The Holy Spirit In You

The Holy Spirit In You

D.L. Moody said, "That which is born of the flesh may die, but that which is born of the Spirit will live forever."

While Jesus was on earth, His disciples walked with Him and sat under His teaching for three and a half years. But the Holy Spirit was never *in them*. Judas was never filled with the Holy Spirit, and none of the disciples were, because Jesus had not yet ascended to the Father's right hand to intercede for us by His blood. The disciples had spent their time with Jesus learning His ways and the way He interacted with the Father. But none of them had received the indwelling of the Holy Spirit.

> *John 14:16-17 - 16 And I will pray the Father, and he shall give you another Comforter, that he may abide with you for ever; 17 [Even] the Spirit of truth; whom the world cannot receive, because it seeth him not, neither knoweth him: but ye know him; for he dwelleth with you, and shall be in you.*

Jesus said this to His disciples, prior to His

crucifixion and resurrection. Then, before His ascension to the right hand of God, He instructed them:

> *Acts 1:4 - 4 And, being assembled together with [them], commanded them that they should not depart from Jerusalem, but wait for the promise of the Father, which, [saith he], ye have heard of me.*

He was speaking of the coming day of Pentecost. The disciples of Jesus did not receive the Holy Spirit at their water baptisms but on the Day of Pentecost. That's why they were commanded by Jesus to wait for the Father's promise!

It was the Birth of the Church, Anno Domini, A.D. 30, in the year of the Lord. On this marvelous Day of Pentecost, also known as Feast of Weeks which takes place 50 days after Passover, as the believers gathered together in one place following the Masters command to wait, they were all of one accord. Suddenly there came a sound. The sound was that of a mighty rushing wind. This was no ordinary wind. It appears to be only the sound of the wind. The sound filled the house, not the wind.

This was the beginning of a new season, when the believers would go deeper and be filled with the Holy

Spirit. The third part of the God Head was now going to be in them.

But this was only the beginning of this miraculous Day of Pentecost. Throughout the Old Testament, fire was often used to show God's presence. The burning bush appeared on Mt. Sinai to Moses when God called him to lead the people of Israel.[15] Fire was also present when the children of Israel left Egypt, as God guided them with a pillar of fire by night.[16] God had also come down to the top of Mt Sinai in fire when He spoke the Ten Commandments to His people.[17]

This day of Pentecost would be no different.

> *Acts 2:3-4 - 3 And there appeared unto them cloven tongues like as of fire, and it sat upon each of them. 4 And they were all filled with the Holy Ghost, and began to speak with other tongues, as the Spirit gave them utterance.*

Fire has a purifying purpose. John the Baptist had said that people would be baptized with the Holy

---

[15] See Exodus 3:2

[16] See Exodus 13:21-22

[17] See Exodus 19:18

Ghost and fire.[18] Fire is a refiner, a purifier, and was used to purge the sin and purify those who were receiving the Baptism of the Holy Spirit. As The fire of the Holy Spirit came down, it separated and came to rest on each of the disciples as they were being made clean.

Another miraculous sign that occurred on the Day of Pentecost was speaking in tongues. Each of the disciples, in amazement, were speaking in "other tongues," showing it was different from their native tongue, and was diverse tongues among them as they gathered in this upper room. This is also referred to as talking in the Spirit, or their prayer language. When you don't know what to pray for, the Spirit will speak for you.[19]

When the disciples moved to the crowded streets, where tourists who had come for the Feast had gathered, they began speaking in the dialect of each one they encountered. They were able to witness for Jesus the Messiah in the languages of those who had come from all nations.

The Holy Spirit *in us*; is a progression. The more we obey God through the promptings of the Holy Spirit, the more of His Spirit He will give to us. Once the

[18] See Luke 3:16

[19] See Romans 8:26

Holy Spirit is in us, we are in a deeper place. We have moved from glory to glory and have walked a little further out into the deep, perhaps up to our waist.

For me, I have a longing for more of God, which is almost fanatical, nothing else satisfies me. At times the feeling is so strong that it becomes overwhelming. It reminds me of Paul when he was blinded and thrown from his horse on the road to Damascus while on his way to persecute the early Christians. Then, when Ananias touched him, as the Holy Spirit had commanded, Paul's sight returned immediately and Paul became almost fanatical in his longing to do the work as he had been commanded. Glory!

We, like Paul, have also been commanded to do the work directed by the Holy Ghost, directed by God the Father! There must be a longing, and a hunger, and there must be a thirst. And that thirst will never be quenched. Many believers, or followers of Jesus Christ, never go beyond the Holy Spirit being in us. But there must be a constant, ongoing infilling of the Holy Spirit.

God's Presence is what transforms us. We must lose sight of ourselves. The presence is God's Glory. The presence will not come where there is evil. God's Presence is Holy. The Holy Spirit is now in us when we believe that Jesus is Lord. As we go deeper out into the water, we draw closer and closer to the things of God and our holy walk with him, we get rid of old sinful habits, make new friends, and leave those who are no longer equally yoked with us behind. This is called the Baptism of the Holy Spirit. We are literally baptized into the third part of the Godhead.

We are becoming the New Man. We live in the visible and invisible existence of two worlds, the natural and spiritual world. In the natural world, we can see, feel, touch, hear, or taste, these are our earthly senses. It is tangible and visible. But the spiritual world we cannot see with our physical eyes, but it is just as real as the natural world. This is where the Holy Ghost, the gifts of the Spirit, and training come in.

Those who have the Holy Spirit can often see angels and have supernatural discernment from God. Moses said to God, "show me your Glory," your attributes, your power, and your presence.[20] The presence of God does not grow, but it is an abiding presence. The power of God does grow, it is faith-driven, and will give you boldness to obey God and keep His commands. The abiding presence is always there, even when you don't feel it.

---

[20] See Exodus 33:18

We have a mighty portion of God dwelling in us. His purpose is that we have a greater fellowship with Him, to enable us to do great works. We have now received power. Power to step out in faith. We are now becoming the New Man that God can use and work through. We will be tested to see if we can hear His voice. We will also begin in different ministries or callings as the Holy Spirit prepares us, showing us our purpose.

Be Ye Holy as I Am Holy

The primary purpose of God for all of us is to be holy. The Holy Spirit is the Spirit of Holiness. According to God's word, He lives within each of us as believers. God has called us to be holy and without blame, we are a holy priesthood and will be presented blameless before God.

Who is Holy? Angels are holy, Apostles and Prophets are holy, believers are holy, children of believers are holy, and the One New Man is holy.[21]

We must be continually filled and full of the Holy Spirit. We must be led and guided by the Holy Spirit, and we are to be sensitive to the Holy Spirit and His leadership.

---

[21] See Acts 10:22; Revelation 18:20; Colossians 3:12; 1 Corinthians 7:14; Ephesians 4:24

People make choices in life, and the choices we make direct our path. The Holy Spirit helps in leading us toward salvation, and He helps direct our path after we are saved. But often we make wrong choices, leading us down the wrong path in life. We can become like the tares or chaff, the weeds, the bad seeds, if we refuse to follow God.[22]

Instead, we must bear the fruit of the Spirit. The Scripture says that those of us who belong to Christ have crucified our flesh in order to walk in love, joy, peace, longsuffering, kindness, goodness, faithfulness, gentleness and self-control.[23]

Those of us that walk in the Spirit and talk in the Spirit, must ask the Holy Spirit to change us into the image of Christ, day by day. We are to pray in the Spirit, obey the Spirit, and receive the unction/anointing of the Spirit. And we are to have faith to step out in what we have been given from God. Faith to accept the authority and power that has been bestowed upon us by God through His Spirit.

It is important that we realize and guard against blasphemy of the Holy Spirit, because this is the *unpardonable sin.*[24] Grieving the Holy Spirit, lying

[22] See Matthew 13:38

[23] See Galatians 5:22-24

[24] See Matthew 12:31-32

to the Holy Spirit, and quenching the Holy Spirit, are also serious offenses.[25] We must walk blamelessly before God. When God says, "Be ye holy as I Am holy..." this is not a suggestion; this is a command.

> *1 Peter 1:16 - 16 Because it is written, 'Be ye holy; for I am holy.'*

My Prayer for Holiness

I had written this prayer many years ago, and have prayed it, as I sought a deeper walk of holiness:

> Lord, I pray that I may be rooted and grounded in love with Christ, who dwells in my heart by faith. Help me, O Lord, to increase in love and abound in love toward my brothers and all other men, even as we do toward You, O Lord. And, that your love may abound, even more in knowledge, and in all judgment.
>
> Let us love one another for you are love, and all of us who love are of God, are born of God, and are love.

---

[25] See Ephesians 4:30; Acts 5:1-4; 1 Thessalonians 5:19

Let us draw closer, O Lord, in kindly affection to my Christian brothers and sisters in love and honor, preferring their company and Christian conversation.

Help me, O Lord, to tame my unruly tongue to think before speaking, and never speaking to intentionally hurt anyone, for we are all made in your image and divine purpose. Let no corrupt communication proceed out of my mouth, O Lord, but only that which is good and edifies others by ministering grace and love to the hearer.

And help me to put off the old man, back when I lived in anger, wrath, malice, blasphemy, and filthy communication. You have touched my soul and the new man has put all old things behind, I give you praise, Lord, I give you honor.

Thank you, Lord, for giving me patience and forgiving those who have come against me, as you have forgiven me, O Lord, so I shall continually forgive them, having no grudge against others.

Help me to put on charity, bound in perfectness, for all who love God must also love our brothers.

If we understand Your Word, O Lord, let us teach with meekness of spirit those who walk under the Law of the Old Testament and help us fulfill the Law of Grace, lifting their burdens. Let us rejoice with those who rejoice and weep with those who weep.

Let us not hold grudges one against another of our brethren, being willing to live honestly.

Let us love not the world, nor the things in it, but love the Lord and one another.

Let us all abstain from sexual thoughts and fornication, keeping your vessel, your body, and mind, clean before God.

I will continually strive, O Lord, toward the mark of holiness set down for us in your Word. Knowing it may only be achieved through love. Love of our Christian brothers and sisters, love of our fellowman, and love of God.

Sincere love, pure love, and godly love - This is Holiness! Amen

Draw closer to the Lord with Holiness, because it is the duty of the believer to be holy. Follow after peace and holiness and try to live a life of purity.

The Spirit-Led Life Begins with Surrender and Obedience.

If you are a believer, you have been "Called" by God. When you have been called by God, He will supply your every need. The importance is in forming a relationship, realizing, He is at your disposal 24/7, through prayer. You pray to the Father, through the Son who is our advocate. You never pray to the Holy Spirit. Always to the Father, and always through the Son.

We must surrender daily and draw near to God. In the New Testament, repentance is a change in one's mind – leading him to turn from evil ways and a changed life. As you receive the Holy Spirit's presence, and follow Him, these seven things from the Book of Romans will occur in your life:

- You will be liberated from sin.
- Righteousness will enter your life in an easy flow of walking after the Spirit.
- Your mentality will be changed as you set your mind on things of the Spirit.
- You will become totally at peace: "to be spiritually minded is peace."
- You will be healed from your head to your toe.
- You will receive the total death to self and total life to God.
- You will receive intimacy with the Father, calling Him, "Abba, Father-Daddy."

Additionally, Jesus said clearly, "My sheep hear My voice." If you are truly His sheep and have received the Holy Spirit, you will hear His voice. You must take time each day to hear the wee small voice of the Spirit. He will open your ears to hear and take the scales from your eyes so you can see. Jesus said many times, "He who has ears to hear, let him hear."

Another purpose God has called all of us to is repentance. To feel sorrow for our wrongdoing and to turn from it. It is a radical change in a person's attitude toward sin. It is a personal decision to turn from sin and follow God. We turn from sin to righteousness.

We are also commanded to forgive others as we have been forgiven by God. Forgiveness is a duty of all who call Jesus their Lord.

Luke 17:4 - 4 And if he trespass against thee seven times in a day, and seven times in a day turn again to thee, saying, I repent; thou shalt forgive him.

An unforgiving spirit is one of the most heinous sins. God will not forgive our unforgiveness, and God does not forgive without repentance.[26]

Matthew 6:15 - 15 But if ye forgive not men their trespasses, neither will your Father forgive your trespasses.

And there are more commands about living with and by the Holy Spirit:

- We are told we are to worship God in spirit and in truth. (John 4:23-24.)
- We are to be fervent in spirit, and we desire to be on fire for the Lord. (Romans 12:11.)
- The value of our spirit is that it can live forever. (Romans 8:10-11.)
- The spirit is more important than the physical. (1 Timothy 4:8.)

Angels are spirits, God is spirit, and man's spirit is housed by a body, a tent.[27] The spirit is the basic part of man's being and it is the spirit that is to be saved

[26] See Matthew 18

[27] See Hebrews 7:14; John 4:23-24; 2 Corinthians 5:1-4

in the day of Jesus Christ.[28] We must surrender ourselves and learn to live by the power of God's Spirit dwelling in us.

The spiritual person lives from their spirit, not from their mind or soul. We need the discerning Spirit, discerning all things. Sometimes, this can be beyond human or soulish judging because it is a mystery. We often live in a different realm with our thoughts, but we are unable to comprehend the things of God and why He gives us such information. By abiding in the presence of the Holy Spirit we can begin to receive all He has for us.

It is not always easy to find other believers that are on the same spiritual level or page that you are on. I praise God that he has sent me four such people. We understand each other and discern on the same level. Of the four, one is a woman, one is my pastor, and two are close friends that I meet with at least weekly either in my home, in a restaurant or on the phone. I pray that God will send more, and that fellow believers will draw closer to God.

We need to come into union with other believers who are of the same mind and heart so that we can communicate on the same level. When we come

---

[28] See 1 Corinthians 5:5

together in unity, there is a sense of quality in the Holy Spirit, a spiritual substance.

Faith & Prayer

It is impossible to accomplish a Christian Life without faith! When faith is in perfect operation in us, we will be in perfect alignment with God. Faith is the measuring stick of our trust and belief in God and the complete Word of God. God is, God always has been, and God always will be.

The Lord has revealed himself throughout nature.

> *Romans 1:20 - 20 For the invisible things of him from the creation of the world are clearly seen, being understood by the things that are made, [even] his eternal power and Godhead; so that they are without excuse:*

We are all called to be faithful. A minister of God must prove themselves to be found faithful.[29] We must live where we can see, hear, and discern our Father's will for our life. We must be obedient to the faith, keep the faith, and strive for the faith of the gospel. We are to edify and unify all believers in the faith until they are conformed to the image of Christ.

---

[29] 1 Corinthians 4:2

Caleb and Joshua were men of courage because they were men of faith. Those who have been greatly used of God in all ages have been men of great faith. The keynote of all our work for God should be: FAITH. Unbelief blocks the blessings from coming into our lives. Where there is union with God, and believers in one accord by His Spirit, a mighty work is always done.

You must believe and share your belief with others. Then, your faith will grow. My God shall supply all my needs, by faith. By faith, I shall diligently seek Him. Speak the Word over your life by faith.

Little is much when God is in it, and we operate in faith. We shall be His witnesses, by faith.

Faith is always followed by courage. The courage that will compel us to move forward and move mountains. Don't wait for others to step out. Be bold. Be a leader, encourage others. Be strong and courageous!

Jesus told His disciples that the things He did, we can do also, and even greater things because He went to the Father. What we need is faith, faith, and more faith. Belief, love, and trust!

We build our faith through confession with our

mouths. Confession is affirming something that I believe. It is testifying of something that I know. It is witnessing for a truth I have believed. Confession of faith with our mouths holds a very large place in Christianity. Jesus planned that this great life and love should be given to the world through testimony, that is, the confession of our lips that Jesus is Lord. Our confession centers around several things:

- First, what God in Christ has wrought for us.
- Second, what God through the Word and the Spirit has wrought in us.
- Third, what we are to the Father in Christ.
- And last of all, that the Holy Spirit has found a spot in each of us.

The Kingdom of God lives in us as we confess His promises. Therefore, I lay hands on myself and on my children as I confess:

- I confess "He will never leave us nor forsake us." (Hebrews 13:5-6)
- I confess that the love of God is shed abroad in my heart by the Holy Spirit. (Romans 5:5)
- I confess "the anointing of the Holy One abides in me." (1John 2:27)
- I confess Jesus as my Lord, and I possess salvation. (Romans10:9-10)
- I confess I lay hands on the sick and they shall recover. (Mark 16:18)

Entering the Presence of God

In time of need, we are to boldly enter the holiest of God's presence by the blood of Jesus.

> *Hebrews 10:19-23 - 19 Having therefore, brethren, boldness to enter into the holiest by the blood of Jesus, 20 By a new and living way, which he hath consecrated for us, through the veil, that is to say, his flesh; 21 And [having] an high priest over the house of God; 22 Let us draw near with a true heart in full assurance of faith, having our hearts sprinkled from an evil conscience, and our bodies washed with pure water. 23 Let us hold fast the profession of [our] faith without wavering; (for he [is] faithful that promised;)*

Through Jesus Christ, God has created a new and living way, which He hath consecrated for us, to enter into the presence of God through the veil that separated us from Him. Christ is not entered into the holy places made with hands, meaning an earthly temple or tabernacle. He entered into heaven itself, and now appears in the presence of God for us! He is our advocate, receiving our prayers in His name, and He offers them to the Father, for then Father God will receive all the glory.

> *Hebrews 9:11-12, 24 - 11 But Christ being come an high priest of good things to come, by a greater and more perfect tabernacle, not made with hands, that is to say, not of this building; 12 Neither by the blood of goats and calves, but by his own blood he entered in once into the holy place, having obtained eternal redemption [for us]. ... 24 For Christ is not entered into the holy places made with hands, [which are] the figures of the true; but into heaven itself, now to appear in the presence of God for us:*

God, the Most High, the Almighty, the holiest of all is now open to us: Christ has opened the way for us into the presence of God.

God is a God of Order

The wonder of God's creations and the order in which things are done is in itself amazing. We must learn to trust God, not man, in times of crisis.[30] God will supply all our needs, according to His riches in glory.[31]

Worship is to honor, revere, adore, give devotion, pay homage, and respect someone, especially God.

---

[30] See Psalm 37:5
[31] See Philippians 4:19

We must learn to worship God according to His instructions. The Tabernacle of Moses is a perfect example of God's perfect order. Through the pattern given for the Old Testament Tabernacle, we are given revelation of how God comes down from Heaven to meet with us and have a place where He can dwell with us.[32] Now, as believers in the New Covenant, we ***are*** the temple of the living God![33]

The Tabernacle is a symbol for the Church, the body of true believers. Designed by God, where His presence is, His Glory. God always has a plan! He has prepared and opened up for us a perfect fellowship with God, access in a life of faith in full union with Christ, and into God's immediate presence. There must be perfect harmony between the place of worship and the worshipper. He has prepared the perfect sanctuary, the holiest of all for us, and the Holy Spirit has prepared us as well.

God is a God of order. All of our services should begin with a true spirit of worship and praise, given in Spirit and in truth. We must allow the Holy Spirit to move and take over our times with God. The believer's spirit is to be in union with the Holy Spirit.[34]

---

[32] See Exodus 25:8

[33] See 1 Corinthians 6:19

[34] See John 4:2—24; Romans 8:16; 1 Corinthians 6:17

Man was created to be a worshipper of God, and it must be done in order: First comes the song, singing and instruments, then the Ministers and Priests to pray and minister.[35] Next is ministering and giving thanks, praising God, ministering in Psalms, rejoicing, clapping, shouting, dancing, lifting up holy hands, ministering in worship, seeking the Lord and the ministering of Amen, meaning so be it.[36] Often when I worship and get lost in Him, I weep because the presence is so strong.

God has a great three-fold principle.

GOD	Father	Son	Holy Spirit
MAN	Spirit	Soul	Body
SALVATION	Justification	Sanctification	Glorification
CLEANSING	Blood of Jesus	Holy Spirit	Water of Baptism
TABERNACLE	Most Holy Place	Holy Place	Outer Court
FEASTS OF THE LORD	Passover	Pentecost	Tabernacles
WORSHIP	Thanksgiving	Praise	Worship
FAITH	Measure of Faith	Fruit of Faith	Gift of Faith

And the list of these sets of three could go on and on. God likes order and He is the author of it. If our

[35] See 1 Chronicles 15:16-27, 23:5; Hebrews 6:19-20
[36] See Psalm 86:17; 1 Chronicles 16:4, 36; 2 Corinthians 1:20

worship and times of meeting together are truly led by Him, they will be done decently and in order.[37]

How to Pray & What to Pray For

It is important to know that the disciples never asked Jesus to teach them how to preach, but their words were, "Lord, teach us to pray." This should always be our prayer.

- Pray for mighty faith and courage.
- Pray that you may bear fruit and continue to grow in God.
- Pray that your daily needs are met.
- Pray for all men to be saved.
- Pray for our rulers.
- Pray for our leaders.
- Pray for deliverance from persecution.
- Pray for the peace of Jerusalem.
- Pray that you be covered by the full Armor of God.[38]
- Pray for Spiritual eyes to see.
- Pray for spiritual discernment.
- Pray that the Father makes known to you His will for your life.
- Pray for the salvation of your family.

Be specific when you pray and make definite

[37] See 1 Corinthians 14:40
[38] See Ephesians 6:14-18

requests. Approach God as Our Father, just as Jesus instructed.[39] Always pray in the name of Jesus because He is our advocate and delivers the prayer to the Father, and the Father will get all the glory. We are never to pray to the Holy Spirit! The Holy Spirit has now prepared us through our faith, to pray in the name of Jesus, to the Father.

When you enter your Prayer Closet, let your heart be clean and right with God. Keep God's Commandments, be pleasing in His sight.

> *Psalm 66:18 - 18 If I regard iniquity in my heart, the Lord will not hear me:*

Throughout our lives, most of us have hidden our pain and suffering. We suppress feelings of fear, hate, hurt, abuse, and misuse. Many of us put on a false front and live a life of pretense. You may fool others, but God knows every hair on your head. This is where your prayer must begin. Recognize your need to be cleaned up. This must be done before the Holy Spirit can live in you.

Confess your sins as they occur, and He will cleanse you from all unrighteousness. Remember, we are not here on this earth only for ourselves, and we never

---

[39] See Luke 11:2

have been. We are here for Him and to fulfill His purpose for us. Each of us who has accepted Christ and is led by the Holy Ghost has purpose.

In our daily prayer, we must ask our Heavenly Father to forgive us, and name the names of those who have hurt us, asking Him to forgive them for what they have done or said to offend us. But if we refuse to forgive others, our Heavenly Father will not forgive us of our sins. When there is unforgiveness in your heart, this can cause the failure of prayers to get through to God.

My Personal Testimony:

Many years ago, I was raped. I had so much hate in my heart for those who had assaulted me. I was obsessed with hate, and even though I did not know their names, their faces lived before me daily.

One day during prayer, I asked God why I felt that He had left me. "Lord I never feel your closeness anymore, why have you left me?" He answered me right away! "I have not left you, but you must forgive those who have hurt you."

I began praying daily, saying that I had forgiven my assailants, my rapists. For months, I prayed this day after day. Still nothing changed. Again, I asked God why He had not returned to me, and again He said, "You must forgive those who have hurt you."

I thought to myself, "But I have forgiven them!" His answer was, "No you have not."

The next day I began seeking my assailants faces and began praying for their salvation. I prayed for each of their salvation because I knew that if they were saved, God would forgive them of their sin. That is what it took. It was as though, now I am back in good graces with my Father, and His presence was back. It was like one thousand pounds had been lifted from me. At that moment I realized that when I forgive others, I am healed. Glory to God!

The Importance of Prayer

You may ask, is prayer really necessary? My answer is yes! Jesus was our example while he was on the earth, He was always praying to the Father. Prayer is vitally important in the life of a Christian. There is a need to communicate, interact and be of one accord with God and with other believers. This is done through on-going prayer.

We are to pray without ceasing, and we are to pray all through life. We are to pray constantly. We are to pray that all men be saved. We are to pray for all rulers and people in government. And pray for all leaders throughout the world. We are to pray day and night. And we are to pray in the Spirit, meaning in tongues. We are also to arise early and pray. We are to pray that we will be restrengthened and pray for healing. Pray that we may conquer our afflictions. Watch and pray for the End Times. And the list goes on and on.

Long prayers are not necessary. But we must pray according to the will of God. Prayer is to be according to the directions in the Bible, according to our personal needs, our heart's cry, and when facing life's trials. Prayers should be prayed in faith, asking for forgiveness, and purity, cleanliness, and obedience. Having set times for prayer will keep us on schedule when essential times are set aside for consistency.

Prayer is the source for receiving all things from God.

> *James 4:2-3 - 2 Ye lust, and have not: ye kill, and desire to have, and cannot obtain: ye fight and war, yet ye have not, because ye ask not. 3 Ye ask, and receive not, because ye ask amiss, that ye may consume [it] upon your lusts.*

The lack of endurance is one of the greatest causes of defeat, especially in prayer. We don't wait well; and have become a society that wants immediate results. If immediate results do not manifest, we give up and pursue something else, figuring, "It must not have been God's will."

But consider that Noah did not see the rain God told Him about until one hundred years after God asked him to build the ark. Not only had he never seen rain in the earth because it had never rained yet, but he also had never heard of rain. But God had spoken and so, he waited.

By perseverance, the tiny snail and the turtles were able to reach the ark! Similarly, as we pray and persist through the power of our faith and belief, there is nothing that can keep us from our miracle of answered prayer.

I have learned that no one is born a prayer warrior. It is the Holy Spirit who shapes us and molds us as he guides us and builds up our confidence. The more we do anything, the better we get at it. Even the disciples walking with Jesus asked the Lord to teach them to pray.

Now that Jesus is ascended to the right hand of God, we can do as He instructed and pray to the Father in

His name. The name of Jesus has authority on earth, and we have a right to use His name. In The Garden of Eden, God walked and talked with Adam and Eve but today, He is walking and talking with us through the Holy Spirit! While Jesus was on the earth, before His ascension, He too walked and talked with His followers. Let us use the mighty name of Jesus in prayer because He has given it us to access the Father this way. He gave us the power of attorney, meaning the authority to use his name against demons or anything that comes against us. Yes, we have the right to use the name of Jesus to cast out and rebuke the devil! We have the right to use the name of Jesus to call out demons that bind men's souls. The name of Jesus is the key, and He has given you and me that key. Hallelujah!

Spiritual Discernment

In the military they strategize to evaluate what is coming against us, and what our retaliation would be. There must be proper training to reach our goals on the road to victory. In order to be properly trained and prepared, it is vitally important that renewed emphasis be put on training and strategies of Spiritual Warfare.

There are two Spiritual Kingdoms in this world that our Churches never seem to talk about: The Kingdom of Satan, who seems to have dominion over this world; and the Kingdom of God, who reigns supreme over all. Our enemy must be exposed. The Bible has forewarned us, and we must first realize there is a great war taking place in the world today.

Unfortunately, the world has fallen under the power of the evil one. The natural man of this world has not received the things of the Spirit of God, for they are foolishness to him. Neither can he know them, because they are spiritually discerned.

> *1 Corinthians 2:14 - 14 But the natural man receiveth not the things of the Spirit of God:*

for they are foolishness unto him: neither can he know [them], because they are spiritually discerned.

We must have spiritual discernment! This world we live in is in direct opposition to God. This world is an evil system, having no hope and being without God. The spirit of this world is in direct opposition to the Holy Spirit. We are in this world but not of it!!!

Galatians 1:4 - 4 Who gave himself for our sins, that he might deliver us from this present evil world, according to the will of God and our Father:

Ephesians 2:12 - 12 That at that time ye were without Christ, being aliens from the commonwealth of Israel, and strangers from the covenants of promise, having no hope, and without God in the world:

2 John 1:7 - 7 For many deceivers are entered into the world, who confess not that Jesus Christ is come in the flesh. This is a deceiver and an antichrist.

John 15:18-19 - 18 If the world hate you, ye know that it hated me before [it hated] you. 19 If ye were of the world, the world would

> *love his own: but because ye are not of the world, but I have chosen you out of the world, therefore the world hateth you.*

Know that people of the flesh and this world hate you! Satan's army uses fear tactics, oppression, and enslavement. But the army of God transforms lives through repentance, conversion, justification, being liberated, set free, and saved. True repentance is a decision and is necessary to avoid Spiritual death.

As believers, we are the Temple of God. We have received the Holy Spirit after accepting Jesus as our Lord and Savior. This is also why it is so important that we all must do the will of the Father through meditating on the Word of God, teaching others the truth, and leading the lost to the cross while teaching them of the glorious Holy Spirit. Let us always know where our strength comes from. Our strength comes from the Lord.

Put on the Armor of God

First, we must all put on the Armor of God before we start the new day.

> *Ephesians 6:11-17 - 11 Put on the whole armour of God, that ye may be able to stand against the wiles of the devil. 12 For we*

wrestle not against flesh and blood, but against principalities, against powers, against the rulers of the darkness of this world, against spiritual wickedness in high [places]. 13 Wherefore take unto you the whole armour of God, that ye may be able to withstand in the evil day, and having done all, to stand. 14 Stand therefore, having your loins girt about with truth, and having on the breastplate of righteousness; 15 And your feet shod with the preparation of the gospel of peace; 16 Above all, taking the shield of faith, wherewith ye shall be able to quench all the fiery darts of the wicked. 17 And take the helmet of salvation, and the sword of the Spirit, which is the word of God:

Do not simply read this and dismiss it as something you were taught in Sunday School or were taught in a church class. This is vital, even more so today than ever before in our country's history, as we approach the end of the world and the coming of that evil day of the wrath of God.

It is important to remember we must "put on" the armor. This takes action on our part, that we may withstand against the wiles of the devil.

Know that the *Helmet of Salvation* protects you from

bondage. The *Sword of the Spirit* is *the Word of God.* Read your Bible daily because it is an offensive and defensive weapon that will defend you in times of need. The *Breast Plate of Righteousness* will protect you from sin and confusion. The *Shield of Faith* will protect you from unbelief and bondage. Also, have your feet shod, meaning be ready! This means reading the Bible and receiving peace from its comforting words, stopping confusion and unbelief.

The Armor of God defends you from the aggression of the world that we live in and protects us from the day-to-day trauma we come in contact with. Jesus used this Armor when He was taken up into the mountain by Satan, trying to prevent Him from stepping out into His ministry.

My Personal Testimony

In the spring of 2016, I had a Ministry called *The House of Prayer, Prophecy and Healing*. We laid hands on the sick and prayed through until they received. We would have different prophets each week exposing church people to the fivefold ministry and gave new ministers the opportunity to preach weekly while building up a following. We assisted in starting three other churches from this location. And this became a "go to place" for other ministers to come and get filled, while worshipping freely and openly.

I had several frequent guests from Africa, most were couples who were nice, strong, Christians. One evening, one of the couples brought a guest from Western Africa. He was very pleasant, and asked if he could return. "Certainly," was my reply. He came several times.

One evening he passed out music CDs to all that were present and gave me one as well. I put it in the music CD player but really didn't care for it. There was a good rhythm but not a church type rhythm and it sounded like sticks or pieces of wood being beaten together. The next evening, he was in attendance, and I heard him make a comment to a woman that was a regular attendee. The comment he made was sexual and very lude. This language had no place in this strongly anointed church! The woman was in tears. I approached this vile man and told him I had heard what he had said, and he was to leave immediately! As I escorted him out the door, I told him he was never to return to my property again. I had no place for vulgar, filthy people who claim to be a Christian. This was a place of Almighty God, and he was never to return again.

The next morning, I was in Patient First, a medical treatment center near my home. After doing all the vitals, they took an X-ray of my lungs. And there it was! Pneumonia in my right lung. They put me on antibacterial medication and asked me to return in nine days. Never before in my life had I had pneumonia. As a matter of fact, I had taken the Pneumonia shot to prevent the disease. I returned to the doctor nine days later and they took x-rays again, this time of both lungs. The right lung had cleared up from the antibacterial medication, but it had jumped over to my left lung!

I went home, threw open my doors, threw open my windows, and went to battle in the spirit, using the name of Jesus. Casting out demons and evil spirits out of my house, off my property, off my street. They could hear me all the way down the street. But when I was finished with that session of prayer, demon spirits had left. That man from Africa had been a witch doctor and he had brought those demons with him! Now those demons were gone through spiritual discernment and prayer in the name of Jesus! Hallelujah! Finally, I called all the people who had received the music CD, and asked them to destroy and discard the witch-craft music.

Always remember: when you lay down with dogs, you get up with fleas. Discernment is needed in all situations as a follower of Christ.

You see my friends, this stuff is real. We have people coming into this country from witch-craft havens.

They now enter into our country and live here. Cover yourself with the almighty Armor of God. Protect yourself, your family, your home. This stuff is real and will kill you. Do not even enter a voodoo or witchcraft store. Do not buy these artifacts and take them into your homes.

> *Ephesians 4:27 ESV - 27 and give no opportunity to the devil.*

I thank God that He has taught me to battle the enemy with the name of Jesus. He has taught me to come against the enemy. People of the evil one are intelligent and subtle, emotional, self-willed, powerful, deceitful, fierce, cruel, and deceptive. Put on your Armor! Put it on daily.

We must learn to use spiritual discernment, for only then will we be able to understand Spiritual things. Pray that God will open your spiritual eyes. In 2 Kings chapter six, there is a story about Elisha's servant Gehazi who was fearful when he saw the great size of the army of Syrians that had surrounded the town where Elisha was staying. Elisha prayed that God would give Gehazi spiritual eyes to see so that he would not be so fearful. God answered this prayer and when the servant looked again, he saw the superior forces of God aligned for battle. This story gives me confidence in two things: 1. Elisha had already known the army of God was lined up because he had spiritual discernment which is why he was praying that his servant Gehazi would receive this ability as well. 2. God can give us this type of spiritual discernment if we ask Him in prayer. Therefore, it should be our prayer that God will also give us spiritual discernment in all matters.

Section Three:

The Holy Spirit Upon You

The Holy Spirit Upon You

Jesus was full of the Holy Ghost when He returned from baptism, and He was led by the Holy Ghost into the wilderness, being tempted by the devil for forty days.[40] Even Jesus, being 100% man and 100% God, needed the Holy Spirit to ward off the devil. The more Jesus was tempted, even from the testing of Satan, the Holy Spirit's power, through Jesus, overcame the temptation again and again, with the power of the Spirit.

Only as we are filled with the Holy Spirit, we too can overcome temptation with the power of the Holy Ghost. We too can receive this same power.

When Jesus came up out of the water at his baptism, he was praying, and the Holy Spirit descended in a bodily shape of a dove. This tells me that the Holy Spirit can appear as different things at different times. Just as the Father became a non- consuming fire in the burning bush.

After overcoming the wilderness temptations of Satan, Jesus began His ministry at the age of thirty,

---

[40] See Luke 4:1-2, 14

filled with the Holy Ghost and with all power, and all authority that had been given Him by the Father. When Jesus stepped out in His ministry, He said, "The Spirit of the Lord is upon Me…"[41] Glory!

We Have Been Given Power

Before His crucifixion and resurrection, Jesus told the disciples that He would not leave them orphans, that He would send the Comforter. And power would come. Jesus had been the Rabbi, the teacher, and the friend to his disciples, for three and a half years. Jesus had healed the sick, opened the eyes of the blind, given the lame strength to walk, raised the dead, expelled demons, and performed many other miracles.

Jesus said, "You shall receive power after the Holy Spirit comes upon you."[42] This is when the revelation begins! The Spirit had come upon the disciples to control and dominate their lives. His presence was clearly seen through a variety of means, they spoke in tongues which was evidence that the Holy Spirit had come upon them. The disciples were now healing the sick. Signs and wonders were taking place. Power was now upon the disciples, and others that the Holy Ghost had touched.

---

[41] See Luke 4:14-16

[42] See Acts 1:8

When they left the upper room and went out into the streets, they were filled beyond measure. Those who were in the crowded streets, visiting the Pentecostal Celebration from many different cities and countries were astounded at what they saw and heard. The book of Luke describes the reaction of the crowd as, amazed and confounded. They marveled, as the people could not understand what was taking place. They soon realized through revelation given by the Spirit that this was the fulfillment of prophecy, quoting Joel 2:28-32, indicating that in these Last Days God was pouring out His Spirit upon all flesh. God was allowing everyone, regardless of race, color, country, or city, to be able to receive the marvelous Holy Spirit, within. The disciples had power, like never before.

> *John 14:12 - 12 Verily, verily, I say unto you, He that believeth on me, the works that I do shall he do also; and greater [works] than these shall he do; because I go unto my Father.*

The greater works of Jesus, to include just a few, are things like: physical healings of the blind, lame and paralytics, the woman with the issue of blood and others that are too numerous to mention. He also changed water into wine; delivered the man possessed by a thousand demons; fed the multitudes of 5,000 and 4,000 with only a few loaves and fish; and raised the dead including the widow's son, Jairus' twelve-year-old daughter, and Lazarus.[43]

Peter and John were filled with the Holy Spirit and power and went to the temple where the crippled man asked for alms. Peter's reply was, "silver and gold have we none, but such as we have, we give to you and the man rose up, walked, leaped, and praised God." Glory!

This same wonderful power has been given to each of us if we ask for it. The Holy Ghost came to live in you at salvation. But you must hunger, you must grow, you must long for more of Him and the power will come. The Lord said, "the things I have done, ***you*** can do also." Do not lose sight of this promise. This is POWER! And it is power that has been given to us for a purpose.

When the Holy Spirit is upon you, He will use you for service. He gives us wisdom and knowledge, all through the Gifts of the Spirit. But you must have faith and pray for a fresh infilling! The Holy Spirit will fill you with power and send you to lay hands on the sick!

---

[43] See John 2:1-11, 11:4, 35-37; Mark 4:41, 5:6-15, 6:34-44, 8:2-9; Lk. 7:16-17, 8:50-56

The Holy Spirit has on occasion sent me to other churches while I was in my family church, and I was asked to lay hands on the sick. And they recovered. You may ask, why would the Holy Spirit do that? Because no one else in the other church had enough faith, or enough power which comes from faith, to even hear the voice of the Spirit, let alone enough power to step out in faith for healing the sick. The fact that I left my church and family to go to another church because the small voice within me had spoken - this is faith! You must move on your faith immediately when the Holy Spirit speaks to you!

On another occasion, during my street ministry, I had a woman in my car because I had taken her to her doctor's appointment. Whenever she was with me, we listened to Christian music and I witnessed to her because she was very hungry for more of God. On the way home from her appointment, as we pulled into her parking spot, she was crying, and said, "Sheila, I want what you have!" Then she said, "I need what you have." At that moment, I reached over and touched her hand saying, "Silver and gold have I none, but such as I have, I give to you!" At that moment, the car was filled with the Holy Ghost! She kept saying "What is that feeling, what is that feeling? O my God, O my God!"

None of this would be possible without the Holy

Spirit. Without the Holy Spirit, there would be no Christianity, for there would be no presence of God, no power or authority from Heaven. The Holy Spirit feeds your thoughts with His power. Faith increases the power, and the power working increases your faith. It is no small thing, to know that we have the same power Jesus has, even greater, because Jesus is our advocate, speaking directly to the Father on our behalf, and the Holy Spirit is in us and upon us. Praise God!

The power comes down from the Father, through the Son, through the Holy Ghost, and pours into us. It only works through your faith, and you must step out in faith. The stronger your faith, the stronger the miracles, signs and wonders will be. Being filled with the Holy Ghost is a constant rejuvenating infilling into our daily lives and can get stronger and stronger. This rejuvenating produces a Christ like attitude and life – to do miracles, signs, wonders and to change our daily lifestyle.

When we are filled with the Holy Ghost, we can feel the Holy Ghost in others. I have no desire to be around those who are not Spirit-Filled, and who are not anointed; unless I am on an assignment for the Lord where, of course, I am around the unsaved to tell them about Jesus. When we are filled with the Holy Ghost, when we are anointed, we are like-minded, and our desire is to speak about the Lord, to praise Him, to enjoy His presence, and to feel His Glory. Our conversation is on point. This is an importance and strength in the fellowship with people who are of one accord. All roads of conversation lead to Christ, there is no time for small-talk, nickel-and-dime conversation, because our conversation turns to worship. It is glorious!

The apostles hid or even denied knowing Jesus at His crucifixion, but after they were filled with the Holy Ghost, they were transformed into outspoken and bold.

> *Acts 1:8 - 8 But ye shall receive power, after that the Holy Ghost is come upon you: and ye shall be witnesses...*

Being baptized with the Holy Ghost means that ***you*** have become a bold witness for the Lord. You have been chosen by God to receive the Holy Spirit. Once you receive this wonderful gift, how much it accomplishes depends on you, the believer. If you are a Christian, be the best that you can be.

Speaking in Tongues

Speaking in tongues is the evidence of the Baptism of the Holy Spirit. It is one of the manifestations of the Spirit being active in a believer's life.[44]

The Scripture says not to forbid speaking in tongues. This means that it is the will of God.[45] Speaking in tongues is profitable to edify and build us up and stimulate our faith. Speaking in tongues also enhances our worship as we praise and magnify God.

The Priestly Anointing

As believers, we are called to be priests and ministers of the Most High God.[46] The priestly anointing is the anointing for ministry and without it, we will not accomplish very much for the Lord. The priestly anointing brings the presence of God, the communion, and the fellowship of the Holy Spirit. Revelation knowledge comes with the priestly anointing. The Holy Spirit is the conduit through which the anointing and power can flow through our ministry and our prayers for others.

As new believers, we are cleansed through the blood of Jesus, born again, and sealed by the anointing of the Holy Spirit. The word Christ is from the Greek word meaning "Anointed One," and the equivalent in the Hebrew means "Messiah."

---

[44] See 1 Corinthians 12:7

[45] See 1 Corinthians 14:37-39

[46] See 1 Peter 2:9

In the Old Testament, anointing was done with oil, ointment, and herbs, or they were anointed with the prayer of faith. There was an official religious anointing of prophets, priests, and kings. For example, in the Old Testament, a leper remained outside the camp until they applied the blood of a sacrifice and then the anointing oil. This made atonement for their sin and cleansed them to join the community of believers.

King Saul was anointed as King by Samuel and wanted the Priestly Anointing also, but he didn't want to wait for God's timing. So, Saul stepped out into that office, but without God. The consequence was that God left Saul. When King Saul lost God's Presence, His Holiness, His Glory, he was without God! This is when the demons entered Saul. Then, Samuel anointed David by pouring a horn of oil on his head to show that God had chosen David to be king.

Anointing in this way can be a pouring, a dab, or a smearing of oil on someone, or something (such as a handkerchief or the hem of a garment), or on a person for healing, or on those that have been chosen to have a purpose or assignment. We can still do this today!

However, the New Testament says, "God anointed Jesus of Nazareth with the Holy Ghost and with power."[47] Jesus is the great High Priest, anointed not by oil but by the power of the Holy Ghost!! We can still use oil to anoint people, but the real anointing is the power of the Holy Ghost when it comes upon us!

For us, the anointing comes upon us for a reason. God will call you for a reason. Don't step out if He has not called you. We can never bring the anointing to others until we have God's love at work in our heart, we must learn to live in the fullness of God's anointing. We must examine our hearts and how we feel towards others. The anointing will not come if there are hard feelings, distrust, grudges, or unforgiveness. Instead, there is an emptiness.

He has commanded unity among us. We are to love one another. There is a special anointing for unity that you can ask the Lord for, and He will pour it out among us. The lack of unity is oftentimes what keeps the anointing from flowing. When believers are together and are of one accord, worshipping, or praising the Lord, the anointing is almost electric. The anointing and unity go together.

When the Holy Spirit is *upon you*, it will be for service to others, which is why your heart must be tender and loving. The Father may give you a Word

[47] See Acts 10:38

of Knowledge to give another or He could use you to lead the lost to salvation. He will use you in miraculous ways, to heal or cast out demons.

We are part of the Army of God, and we must learn to recognize His voice. The Holy Spirit now lives within us and for special assignments, He comes upon us so that we will fulfill the will of the Father. He has prepared you for service and is getting ready to send you out. You will feel inadequate but have no fear, He will supply all your needs. Once your assignment has been completed, you will feel so excited and proud that God called you, and He used you. God gave you an assignment and helped you to complete it successfully! Wow! What a great God!

How far you go with God and how deep you go with Him, is up to you! Be obedient, be timely, be respectful, and in all that you do, do it to honor the Father.

When I became filled with the Holy Ghost, my life changed drastically. Being filled with the Holy Ghost draws people to you, as though they can see the light of the Lord shining in you and through you. The Spirit will send you to strangers, to meetings, restaurants, to the mission field – anywhere at any time. He might put you in embarrassing situations, but you always come out on top! Even though Jesus is the Head of the Church, and all things are done in

His name, it is through the Holy Spirit that all things are carried out. And the Holy Spirit glorifies Christ in all that He does.

Relating to the Holy Spirit & Power

The human body and mind cannot produce the Christian life without the Holy Spirit. The Holy Spirit begins in our life by being *with us*, preparing us for salvation. Then, later he is *in us* at salvation and depending on our spiritual growth, He may come upon us for service.

Throughout my life, the Holy Spirit has been a star player in my growth in the Lord. He has changed my walk, my attitude, the way I deal with others, and my career choices. I have experienced numerous spiritual revelations since I was filled with the Holy Ghost. As I continue to serve Him, I am determined to continue to grow by leaps and bounds by staying in the Word of God, praying in the Spirit, asking for spiritual discernment, putting on the Armor of God daily, witnessing to the lost, helping those in need, and staying close to those special like-minded people that God put in my life, that we may continue to grow together.

In my life, I have found that there are four different ways the Holy Spirit relates to me:

1. Through the Word of God, reading about the works of the Spirit in every book of the Bible, Old Testament and New Testament.

2. From the testimonies of fellow Christians as they share their personal experiences with the Holy Spirit.

3. Through reading books on the Holy Spirit written by others throughout the world.

4. Through private revelation, dreams, visions, mystical phenomena, charismatic phenomena, miraculous transport, interventions, and discernment of spirits which are all, I believe, given for the good of the individual or for others in the Church.

By far, I have been most impacted by my personal experiences with the Holy Spirit. In this section, I hope to convey the many wonderful attributes of the Holy Spirit that I have collected during these years of obsessed study and have experienced personally.

Throughout the Bible, we find that the Holy Spirit has a personality. The Holy Spirit is a person with personality, a nature, and He is God, an equal member of the Godhead. He does things for us including, but not limited to:

- He Speaks (Acts 28:25)
- He Teaches (John 14:26)
- He Strives with Sinners (Genesis 6:3)
- He Comforts (Acts 9:31)
- He Helps our Infirmities (Romans 8:26)
- He is Grieved (Ephesians 4:30)
- He is Resisted (Acts 9:51)

All the attributes mentioned are interwoven in our daily lives as we walk with Jesus. Many times, these interactions with the Holy Spirit go unnoticed but whether detected or not, the Holy Spirit is more real than anything. Once you receive the fullness of the Holy Spirit, you will know it for yourself.

In 1 Corinthians 2:14-15 in the Dake Bible, man is described as being either a "Natural Man" or a "Spiritual Man." The *Natural Man* is a person, male or female, who is living under the control of the fleshly passions. This is the sensual and deprived part of humanity in contrast with the rational part.[48] He is the natural/animal man as opposed to the *Spiritual Man*. He has no sense of spiritual values and no relish for them. He counts it the highest wisdom to live for this world and carnal pleasures. Spiritual things are foolishness to him. He cannot see their supreme excellence due to his animal appetites and being

---

[48] See Galatians 5:19-21; Romans 1:29-32; 1 Corinthians 6:9-11; Colossians 3:5-10

spiritually dead.[49]

In contrast, the *Spiritual Man* is a person living under the control of the Holy Spirit who minds the things of the Spirit.[50] This person has the mind of Christ and discerns and esteems spiritual things above the sensual as a new creature who has been resurrected from spiritual death in trespasses and sins to new life in Christ. [51]

Jesus poured out the Holy Spirit so that we as believers can function as the *Spiritual Man*. We have the same Spirit as GOD! Praise God! When we put our faith in Jesus and receive the Holy Spirit, we have the Holy Spirit of God living inside of us.

This said, to be filled with the Holy Spirit for service, you can ask for it. You can ask in the privacy of your home or during a service at church and receive it from God. Ask for the fullness of the Spirit and it shall be given to you. It shall be given with the evidence of speaking in tongues.

The most wonderful thing in this life is accepting Jesus Christ as Lord and Savior of your life, followed

---

[49] Ephesians 2:1-9

[50] See 1 Corinthians 2:15, 3:1, 9:11, 14:37, 15:44-46; Romans 8:1-13; Galatians 5:16-26

[51] See 2 Corinthians 5:17-18; Ephesians 2:1-9, 4:22-24

by being infilled with the Holy Ghost with evidence of speaking in tongues.[52]

This happened for me after I read the life story of Smith Wigglesworth. It was a very small pocket-sized book. The next morning, I picked myself up off the floor, not knowing what had happened. I felt warm oil running over my head and down my back and back again three times before I could pull myself up. I thought I was going to die. Yet I knew it was of God.

While attending the Baptist Church, I never heard of these types of things happening. I thought that when you accepted Christ as your Savior, you received the Holy Ghost, once and for all. I had not been taught that the Holy Spirit was with you for salvation, and He is in you for continued growth, and upon you for service to others.

But now it was crystal clear. I asked for the holy language of tongues and received it. I spoke only a few words at first, but it is something you must practice. The more you spoke in tongues, the more natural it became. I had never heard anyone speak in tongues before, but when I asked God for it, He gave it to me. And if you keep asking, He will give it to you.

---

[52] Acts 2:1-13; 4:1-5; 10:44

Power and How It Grows

For seven years I sat under the teaching and powerful anointing of a very famous man of God. Traveling from conference to conference all over the mid-eastern part of the United States. Traveling from conference to conference, living and breathing every word he spoke and taught, including traveling to Israel with His ministry family. Sitting on the bank of the Sea of Galilee as he preached sermons from that beautiful location under a mighty anointing, I could feel the anointing that was upon me grow as I continued in my hunger for more and more of God.

Just as in the Garden of Eden when God walked and talked with Adam, so is the unmistakable presence of the Holy Spirit with us today, but He is also *in us* and *upon us*! How marvelous, how wonderful is His love for us! We have been given the authority and the power and the charge to do the will of the Father in this world.

Kathrine Kuhlman once said, "Lord, please don't take the Holy Spirit from me." This would be my cry today, tomorrow, and forever. I love and treasure Him so. He has become my life, and I pray, "Lord, please don't ever take the Holy Spirit, nor your presence from me. In the Holy name of Jesus."

John 7:38 tells us about rivers of living water coming out of our inmost being. This is the power of the Holy Spirit. Ezekiel 47 talks about the water that flows from God's house, the Temple. In verse 3, the water was to the ankles, verse 4 it was to the knees, next it was deep enough to swim in. We are called to go deeper into the depths of the Spirit of God. The closer we are to the anointing, the heavier our anointing becomes. That is the power, and that power can grow.

In Acts 1:8 we see the power grew through persecution. The greater the persecution, the greater the power. Acts 2:47 tells us they *added* to the church, then *multiplied*. In Acts 6:7, they *added greatly* to the church and then *grew without number*.

The power has many purposes, but witnessing of Jesus and the Gospel is the most important purpose of the power. Each time we step out in this power to witness of Jesus, our power grows. The power grows the more you feed it!

Below are seven ways this power can grow:

Related Verse	**Through**	**Additional**
Acts 10:44	Hear the Word	Hunger & Thirst
Acts 5:12	One Accord/ Unity	Oneness
Acts 14:8-10	Faith	Brings Miracles
2 Kings 3:15	Worship	Worship is not Praise
Acts 4:29-34	Prayer	Brings the Power of God
Acts 4:13	Association	One sinner destroys much good
Mark 6:47-48	Seek the Lord	Contain Him (Luke 24:13-26)

Hear the Word of God, read the Word of God, listen to the Word of God, and be fed by the Word of God. Attend a church where you are fed with the Word of God. Take notes and review your notes. Make sure they align with the Word of God.

Unity, oneness, one accord, when two or three are gathered in the name of Jesus. In the Upper Room, they were of one accord. The same thought, the same heart, and the oneness of all those who were present.

Faith is believing what the Word of God says. Belief in all that has been said and promised. Without doubt.

Worship, the secrets of your heart made manifest of unspeakable love, that pours out through your inner soul and heart to the God you love above all else.

Prayer, spoken or silent, in your native tongue or spiritual tongue. A form of adoration,
requests, spoken to Our Father, through our Advocate the Son. Prayer without ceasing, from your heart through your mind, at all times throughout the day or night.

Association: Look at the heart and the intent of those around you. One sinner can destroy much good. Avoid the influence of those you are not familiar with. Sit under the teaching of an anointed minister. Impartation follows a mighty anointing. Distance yourself from those who walk in sin. The Lord said, "Be ye Holy, as I am Holy." Associate with those who carry a mighty anointing. Elisha's double anointing came down from Elijah, through his mantel. Choose your friends and associates carefully and wisely!

Seek Him! Seek the Lord, for He truly loves to hide, it is His nature to hide, though He loves to be found. Pray, "Lord, please don't pass me by!"

Spiritual Gifts Working By the Holy Spirit

This spiritual realm that we are now privy to is alarmingly fantastic, somewhat like working for the Secret Service. Only better!

When we are born physically, we possess certain natural abilities. When we are born again spiritually, we receive spiritual gifts, and the Holy Spirit works through us supernaturally. Spiritual gifts are an expression of "the manifold grace of God."[53] Just as there are many gifts, there are many ways to organize them for study and application.

When we are called of God and walk faithfully in that calling, often we will be given several Spiritual gifts. Then there are the gifts of the Word of Wisdom, the word of knowledge, the discerning of spirits, the gifts of healing, the gift of faith at any given time or situation, the working of miracles, the gift of prophecy, and the gift of tongues, and the gift of interpretation of tongues. At any given time or situation, whatever gift we need is at our disposal.

---

[53] See 1 Peter 4:10

God knows what we need and will supply it. Ask, and it shall be given. When we are called to fulfill an assignment, He will supply our every need.

Many Christians wonder about their spiritual gifts, and how to effectively use them. We are instructed in Romans 13:8, "Owe no man anything, but to love one another for He that loveth another hath fulfilled the Law." As servants of God, we should yield our members to righteousness and holiness, living free from sin, receiving and functioning in the God-given gifts for the perfecting of the saints and for the work of the ministry. The Holy Spirit unites with our spirit and works through us to achieve God's supernatural goals. The Holy Spirit gives us the desire and power to do the will of God.

Most of the problems and frustrations come by trying to activate the gifts from the flesh rather than from the energizing power of the Holy Spirit. But as we exercise our gifts, we experience personal fulfillment and a sense of joy. By concentrating on our gifts, we achieve maximum fruitfulness and reap a sense of fulfillment and purpose in helping others.

God is a giver! God has given us Salvation, for it is a gift from God.[54] We are saved by Grace. He has

[54] See Ephesians 2:8

given us the gift of peace, the gift of grace, and He has given us the ability to minister in His name.

> *James 1:17 - 17 Every good gift and every perfect gift is from above, and cometh down from the Father of lights, with whom is no variableness, neither shadow of turning.*

Visions Compared to Dreams

A vision has the meaning of something mentally seen, or an actual appearance or form. It can be an apparition, or something actually gazed upon, an external inspired appearance. This means that visions usually take place in an awakened state, not when we are asleep. It is like a direct illumination from God that breaks through and lets us see the spiritual realm around us. Of course, we do not see everything in that realm, only what the Lord chooses for us to see. When He gives us a vision, there is a purpose. There can also be a vision within a vision.[55]

Dreams on the other hand have subtle differences. The Bible Greek text says a dream is something that appears or is seen in sleep. An important difference between a vision and a dream is that visions often, but not always, show us something that is actually

---

[55] See Zechariah 5:5

happening around us, or will appear in the near or not too distant future. Dreams, however, seem to be generally for the "curing" of the soul, alerting us of things to come or something we need to rectify.

Both visions and dreams can be examples used to bring a warning. Visions are more to alert you of an impending danger or accident, so we can intercede. Only those who have "eyes to see" can appreciate what is going on in the eternal realms.

Visions occur four times as much as dreams. Dreams can take about 20% of our sleep time. The dreams that are remembered most are those that occur just prior to wakening. For example, in the story of Jacob's dream about the ladder, Jacob arose early at dawn having just recalled his dream.[56]

When God gives us the dream, He is most likely to give us the meaning as well. This said, future revelation can be dependent on our present obedience.

The Five-Fold Ministry

Missing from the Spirit-Filled churches of today are the Five-Fold Ministries. These gifts are the Apostle,

[56] See Genesis 28:18

Prophet, Evangelist, Pastor and Teacher. Each with them has its own personal calling from God. Specific duties, each holding a special office to help edify the church. Each is Spirit-Filled and guided by the Holy Spirit.

It is each of the Five-Fold Ministry's responsibility to fulfill their calling, teaching the church to walk out the perfection of their faith. We are to be complete and perfect when Christ returns for His church, a Bride without spot or wrinkle. Being of one mind in peace and love, being complete and perfect, as we walk out the perfection of our faith.

So, what is missing from The Five-Fold Ministry of today?

The *Evangelist* who works to get the people saved. They tell of the Gospel of Jesus, the Cross, and the Blood. The *Evangelist* introduces the release of the miracles, signs and wonders in the church and works with the Holy Spirit to lead the lost to salvation. The *Evangelist* introduces the new convert to the *Pastor*.

However, in many churches, the *Pastor* is also missing from the church. He has become the teacher, even though he is supposed to be the shepherd to God's sheep. The *Pastor* is to nurture the sheep of his flock and show them how to follow the covenant.

The Pastor provides comfort, care, and protection. The *Pastor* is there to encourage the growth of the Christian, from glory to glory, and from immaturity to maturity. Explaining our true purpose, and how to get there, tenderly loving us every step of the way.

The true role of the *Teacher* is missing as the one who provides instruction and training. Real *Teachers* are called by God, and they are Spirit-Filled, with the Pentecostal-type experience. They hunger and thirst for more of God, and they long to tell others of the truth of God’s Word. Teachers provide instruction, understanding, and ongoing training so that all believers can be edified.

The *Prophet* is missing who gives us visions and direction. Where is the *Prophet?* He is everywhere! A true prophet is called by God. He is the mouthpiece of God, through the Holy Spirit. When God speaks, he speaks. He does not elaborate. He speaks what God speaks. A true prophet is not a personal prophet for each individual person in the church but has spiritual discernment and a direct line from the Father.

The *Apostle* is missing. Their role is to establish the church and set it in order so every Christian can be equipped to minister in God's power.

Numerous times I have been asked my opinion on what is needed most in today's churches. My answer is always the same. The most needed thing in today's church is the Five-Fold Ministry and holiness!

Please understand that God uses clean vessels. This means people who have purified their lives and are living to be holy as God is holy. Those who are chosen by God need to grow to maturity and perfection in order to fulfill their calling. We are to leave the elementary doctrines of Christ. We are to be wise, be made perfect. We are to cherish what God gives us.

But unfortunately, many churches have become a place for power-hungry preachers to glorify themselves, while earning a substantial income, using his/her gift for gab, oratory, or theatrics to "succeed" in this life. But in truth, many have strayed greatly from the true Gospel.

The growth of the church has failed because of the lack of *Evangelists*. Instead, homespun books written by the preacher have taken their place, again trying to make a name and some money for the preacher. What happened to the alter call? The call to salvation? What has happened to the alter call for the Baptism in the Holy Spirit?

The growth of the churches has drifted from the faith because of the lack of leadership and spiritual discernment from the *Apostle. Many* of these so-called apostles were never called by God, but have been called by man. Sometimes, the person has taken a class where they had to pay for the training to become an Apostle. This is not how it works. These are gifts from God alone.

But there is hope because some people in the church do have revelation about this. God will bring it to pass! Glory!

Personal Testimony of the Five-Fold Ministry

I was at the hair-dressers one Saturday morning and joined in on a conversation going on with another hair stylist who was talking about her church. After giving testimonies and sharing our love for the Lord, she invited me to her church. We exchanged names and numbers and promised to keep in touch. That afternoon, I attended a *Prophets Round Table* meeting at my church and told them of my new encounter with the beautician. Later that evening the woman called me at home and invited me again to her church, saying she had spoken to her Pastor, and he was looking forward to meeting me.

The next morning, I arrived at the church fifteen

minutes early, only to find I was the only one there. I then noticed three other cars pulling into the church parking lot. I laughed to myself when I noticed the Apostle from my church, one of the Pastors, and a Prophet. Of course, I was the Evangelist and Teacher. Remarkably, we had the whole Five-Fold Ministry in place without the knowledge of the other.

The Pastor of this church arrived late because this was his Sunday to pick up others in the community, and he apologized for being late. After the opening prayer the Church Pastor called me out by name and ask me to introduce myself and those that had come with me.

I introduced them by name and telling of the office they held. I said, "We are the Five-Fold ministry." Remember, this was not planned, this was a God moment. The Pastor then called each one out by name, and they explained what the responsibilities of the office they held where according to the Word of God. It was a true God moment, and the entire congregation knew it. This was so exciting, and God had orchestrated this wonderful moment in time. He was showing us what was missing in the church of today.

Section Four:

My Story & Experiences with the Holy Spirit

My Story & Experiences with the Holy Spirit

My father was Jewish and my mother Catholic but neither of them attended services. There was never a Bible in our home! My mother had a Catholic book of prayers, called a Catholic Missal. She read this book daily, praying the prayers of others, always to herself, and she never shared the book with us.

Seven years after my father returned from World War II, he went through the court system and legally had our last name changed from Goldberg (his birth name) to his mother's maiden name, a non-Jewish name. My father feared persecution upon our family because most of our family had lived in Goldberg, Germany, and were murdered or sent off on the trains to camps and they never returned! You can understand my father's intention to protect us from this fate by steering us away from our Jewish heritage.

When I was twenty years old, my first son was born. He was born with birth defects, caused from an abusive marriage. He passed away without ever leaving the hospital. That evening there was a knock at our door. A friend of my husband's, an evangelist, stood there and told my husband that they wanted us both to join them for the evening. So, we went. We were shocked when we were taken to a Southern Baptist Revival. We didn't have a clue about these things because both of us were totally unchurched.

I sat there with tears pouring down my face, knowing that every word the preacher was speaking was aimed directly at me. I stood to my feet to walk down the aisle toward the front of the sanctuary. My husband grabbed my wrist and yanked me back while he murmured under his breath with teeth clenched, "Don't you embarrass me!" The evangelist, who was like a father figure to my husband, said to him, "Let her go." And he did.

Days later, several women from the church came over to talk with me. But my husband sent them away and they never returned. My husband had the same opportunity as I did, to accept Christ or not. To my knowledge, he died without ever accepting Christ as his savior.

Nevertheless, this was the beginning of my new life with Christ. Years earlier, I had accepted Jesus as Lord and Savior by watching Evangelist Billy Graham on his weekly television program but this time, it was real. The Bible they gave me the night of the revival made it real to me. The hunger and yearning that had been locked up within me my entire life was now breaking loose. I could feel the Holy Spirit within me, showing me where to go in the Word of God. I began memorizing the tribes of my people, Israel. Then, I memorized them in alphabetical order. I would lay in bed at night going over everything that I had learned that day, while reviewing what I had learned before. It was glorious!

Talking to the Holy Spirit became my favorite pastime, day and night. He had become my best friend. I read every word I could about Him. I read where he creates, renews, convicts, and performs miracles. I read about how we are supported by and filled by, offered to God by, raised by, and justified by the Holy Spirit.

Here are some of the many experiences I have had where I know that the Holy Spirit intervened in my life.

1. Miraculous Phenomena

The Holy Spirit led me to Chapter 17 of Genesis. As I read and reread that chapter, I saw where Abraham fell upon his face and laughed when God told him that Sarah would bear him a son at one hundred years old. I could see why Abraham laughed but I began to laugh because of the verses where Abram and Sarai had their names changed by God. Their son who was to be born would be named Isaac, which means laughter, at the same time that God changed their names using the letters HA-HA! God has such a great since of humor!

As I sat reading my Bible and laughing, the Holy Spirit spoke to my Spirit saying, “I have changed your name too!” I answered, “O Lord, what have you changed it to?” He told me to write my name and so I wrote my name SHEILA clearly on the pad of paper. Then He asked me, “What do you see?” My response was, “I see Sheila?” He told me to write it again, so I did. A third time He said, “Write your name,” and I began to write, but each time I added a letter to my name, the letter was moved. Each letter kept on moving until the name spelled ELISHA, using each letter in my name. I realized at that moment that my name had been changed, and my Jewish heritage had been restored by using the name Elisha as my new name, given by God. The meaning of Elisha is, “my God is salvation”. The mantle of Elijah was cast on Elisha being a symbol of prophetic succession and power when it fell on Elisha from Elijah, who mysteriously made his exit from this life on the banks of the Jordan River.[57] Elisha asked Elijah for a double anointing and performed exactly double the miracles as Elijah had.

[57] See 2 Kings 2:8-11

2. A Prophetic Miracle

My teenaged daughter had been invited to spend two weeks of her summer vacation at a farm of the grandparents of her best friend, in West Virginia. When she asked me if she could go, I felt the Holy Spirit telling me, "NO." It was an unction, what I call a movement in my left side, beneath my rib cage.

Nevertheless, I told my daughter I would pray about it and get back with her. Later, my daughter asked again if she could go. At that moment the Holy Spirit was very clear and said, "Don't let her go!" I told her she could not go and explained to her why not. She was very upset!

Two weeks later, on the front page of our county newspaper was a picture of a burnt car with headlines "Family of Four, Plus One, Burn to Death as Gas Tank Explodes." They were rear-ended by a trash truck that ignited the gas tank of the car. The mother, her two daughters and son, plus the extra guest that went in my daughter's place all were pronounced dead.

3. God Confirmed My Calling to Teach

It was 7 a.m. on a Monday morning. I began Bible study with prayer. Then suddenly, as though there was someone sitting with me, I heard the audible voice of God say, “You are to TEACH.” At 9 o’clock, I called my pastor and told him that God had called me to Teach, and I asked him what I should do.

Then, these things happened successively in the days and weeks that followed:

- The following Sunday, I began teaching a new women’s class called Ruth’s Love.
- Three weeks later, I received a call from the College of Southern Maryland asking me to teach Food Sanitation Certification Classes at the college.
- Three months later I was called by University of D.C. to teach Food Sanitation classes as outreach throughout the D.C. area, teaching the Word of God to the under-privileged people in the four different sections of Washington, D.C.
- For the past twenty-four years, I have been privileged to teach outreach, preach and minister in various places, wherever God sent me.
- I have become a Stephens Ministry Teacher, teaching in the prison system throughout the area where I live.
- Recently I have been asked to train the trainers in the Stephens Ministry in Maryland. I will venture out into the Stephens Ministry when I complete my degree program. Knowing there is so much writing involved, I don’t want to overload my time.

To this day, I continue to teach and "train the trainer," preparing my students to also become teachers. Plus, I am currently attending Destiny Bible College, working toward my Doctorate degree, through Word of Life International Church. I continue learning and growing in my own knowledge and understanding of God so that I may continue to teach in fulfillment of God's call upon my life while touching the lives of others.

God has also "Called" me to be an Evangelist. I have led many people to the Lord, both in groups and often as individual settings.

4. Infused Mystical Knowledge

On the ninth of September 2001, my husband and I attended a Sunday evening Bible study at the First Baptist Church of St Charles. My husband was a deacon there and I taught the women's Bible study class. It was a small Sunday evening class, and we gathered on the right side of the church with about fifteen people.

As Pastor Bill was teaching his class, I noticed something from my peripheral vision to the left. In the center of the back wall, on the altar was an eight-foot golden oak cross which was tastefully lit and quite beautiful. Instead of focusing on Pastor Bill, my eyes were being drawn to the cross where I saw a vision of blood pouring down into the baptismal pool below the cross. I began to weep!

The pastor asked me, "Sheila, what is wrong?"

I told him I knew it wasn't real, but I saw what I saw! Everyone turned to see, but of course the vision was only for my eyes to see.

But what I had seen was very real. The blood I saw was pouring from the cross into the baptismal pool that was directly below the cross. "Sheila, you have had a vision," the Pastor said. I asked him what that meant, and he explained that visions can be good or bad and that we must pray for or against what God is revealing through the vision.

We all began to pray, not knowing that it was a warning about the events that were about to take place two days later on September 11, 2001.

Once the tragedy of 9/11 happened, the Pastor called me that morning to confirm the purpose of the vision that I had seen. What I had seen in the spirit was the blood of those who had died as of the result of the attack on the Twin Towers in New York that Tuesday morning at 8 a.m., where thousands died.

5. Supernatural Spiritual Cleansing

I went to two o'clock prayer in my prayer closet. A swirling brilliant white light entered my right eye in the shape of a funnel cloud turning in a clockwise motion. It was cool, refreshing, and beautiful. I could faintly see small amounts of emerald-green as the funnel continued to turn for 30 seconds. Then, it entered my left eye in the same exact way that it had entered my right eye. It also lasted 30 seconds and exited out toward the north.

That night as I went to sleep, I was awakened with spiritual sludge, mud, silk, and filth all being flung from my eyes into the atmosphere. It was like something seen in a Star Wars movie. It looked like small particles of filth, but I knew it was sin. I also knew I didn't want to identify it. After this was finished, I went into a peaceful sleep.

When I woke up the next morning, it was beautiful. I knew that something had entered my body during the whirlwind and that as I slept, my body was purged, and stripped of everything filthy. I realized that it was impossible for the Holy Spirit to dwell in my body until I was purged of all sin. Nothing unclean will enter heaven.[58]

---

[58] See Revelation 21:27

6. Miraculous Transport and Prophecy

I was sitting on the edge of my bed reading the Bible. Suddenly, I was lifted up and taken to a location that I was very familiar with. I was in Congress Heights in Southeast D.C., just at the top of Portland Street and MLK Ave. I was standing on the sidewalk in front of where the Pizza Carry Out used to be, looking down toward Bolling Air Base. There was a large group of militant-looking people gathering with their teenage sons, and they were all dressed in fatigue uniforms, carrying automatic weapons.

I recognized many of the activists as students from my classes, most of whom had graduated into the workplace. It appeared to be a meeting place upstairs in the building where I was standing. The leader, who was standing across from me with two of his sons, had been in several of my classes and we had enjoyed a good working relationship. I cried out, "Where are you going, what are you doing?" He turned and began to walk away. Again, I cried out even louder than before, "Where are you going and what are you doing?" He told me, "We are gathering from the four points of the capital, north, south, east, and west. They are coming from Maryland by way of South Capitol Street; from Virginia by way of 14th Street Bridge; from Prince Georges County by way of Pennsylvania Avenue; and from the beltway by way of North Capital Street. We are taking down the Capital, we are taking down the White House." They began marching off toward the South Capitol beltway as I began to weep. When I dried my eyes, I was transported back to my home, sitting on the bed with my Bible. "Lord," I said, "What am I to do?" "Pray," is what I heard.

The Holy Spirit said, "This vision has not yet come to pass. We must continue to pray against this take over."

7. Cures and Miraculous Healings

It was Sunday morning and I had just finished my Ruth's Love women's class, so I was going to the sanctuary for service. My husband was the deacon of the week, and I was going to meet him there. I took my seat and began praying. Suddenly, the Holy Spirit had a job for me to do. When my husband came over and sat down, I told him God had just asked me to go to the Assembly of God Church at Cedarville, Maryland, which was only about 15 minutes from my church. "What for?" he asked. I replied, "He wants me to lay hands on the man with prostate cancer at that Church," using the Holy Spirits wording. My husband said, "He what?!?" Anyway, he gave me directions to the church, and I went.

As I entered the church, there were about twenty-five to thirty people in attendance. While I was being welcomed by many people, I scoped out those in attendance because I was looking for someone who may be sick.

Suddenly, the keyboard player came out and service was about to start. As he was playing chords on the piano, he began talking as he played. He said, "I want to thank you for the cards, the delicious covered dishes, your prayers and for helping my wife." At that moment I stood up and asked, "Sir, could you tell me what is wrong with you?" His facial expression said it all; it said, "Who are you, and do I want to tell you anything this personal?" It seemed to take him a while before he answered me, but when he did, he said, "I have prostate Cancer!" I immediately replied, "No sir, you ***had*** prostate cancer. Almighty God has sent me here this morning. He had me leave my church and family, to come lay hands on you!"

It took this man an instant to get the anointing oil and run down the aisle to where I stood, surrounded by those in attendance. As they laid hands on me and I laid hands on him, I anointed him saying, "In the name of Jesus Christ of Nazareth, you are healed!"

This man was the son of the church pastor, one of the

most powerful preachers I know. Yet God brought me from across the county to lay hands on his son. He was completely healed.

8. A Word of Knowledge; And A Prayer of Reward

After attending a three-day healing seminar sponsored by Randy Clark Ministries in Fredericksburg, Virginia, I said my goodbyes and started out for the hour-long drive home to Waldorf, Maryland. Less than one mile into my trip, the Holy Spirit said, "Pull into this restaurant." At the light I turned right, pulling into the lot at the Chili's eatery on the corner. As I entered the front door of the restaurant, they immediately ushered me to a two-seater table.

I placed a simple order of salad and iced tea, knowing that eating was not my main function here. I began looking around to see what the Holy Spirit had in store for me.

It was the Christmas season, and the decorations were very festive. There was a family sitting somewhat across from me that looked to me like a Rockwell painting. They also looked as though they had just taken their Christmas photo at the Olin Mills Studios. The little one year old was all dressed up in a red velvet dress, and the grandmother was feeding her crackers to keep her still, as we parents do. The child was in a highchair pulled up to the table. Granddaddy sat next to his wife and across from them were the mom and dad. All were dressed in coordinating seasonal colors.

The waitress brought my order, and I began sipping on the tea as I continued looking around with expectancy. Suddenly, the Holy Spirit said, "Go over to that table, tell them to get the crackers off the table because the tiles they are laying on have red dye in them, that may be poisonous." To this, my response was, "What?!?" I could not believe this was my assignment! Again, the Holy Spirit repeated to me verbatim what He had said before. I could feel His hand gently nudging me out of the booth as I headed in the direction of their table.

I reached out and touched grand-mom on the shoulder, "Pardon me, I know you're going to think I'm crazy but, God just spoke to me and asked that I warn you that the tiles on the table have red dye in them and could be poisonous!" She never made eye contact with me, but she quickly went about cleaning up the crackers. She then placed a napkin on the table and gave fresh crackers to the child. I turned and went back to my seat, motioned for the waiter to bring my check, as I reached for my wallet.

I felt very foolish! As I was leaving, I stopped by their table to apologize for interrupting their lunch. This time, the child's father, who was a very distinguished looking gentleman, said to me, "I thank you for your boldness. Few people would have delivered such a message. The message was not for my mother but for me. I am Rev.--- of the First Baptist Church of Fredericksburg and I have been questioning God on whether he still talks to His people. He used you today to prove that He does indeed talk to His people and uses them for His purpose." I smiled and thanked him.

Walking away, I felt a smile on my face and thanked God for using me to give a Word of Knowledge to this mighty Preacher. I knew his church was the biggest one in Old Town Fredericksburg, Virginia.

As I walked toward my car, I smiled at the young man sitting on the bench because he had been there when I entered the restaurant. I was in amazement at what had just taken place. I started the ignition of my car and felt someone staring at me. So, I turned and there stood this young man from the bench. Cracking the window about two inches and making sure the door was locked, I then asked him, "May I help you?" He answered, "I feel led to pray for you!" I found the word "led" to be a strange choice of words. I put the window down, placing my left arm on the open space, for him to touch and make contact as he prayed.

Suddenly without any words or warning, there was a second person standing there. He was much taller and darker than the first. Both of them placed their hands on my arm and began praying. Their prayer was beautiful, I listened intently and began to cry as they continued for at least three minutes.

When they had finished, without a word, they turned together and walked toward the restaurant and then entered. I heard the Holy Spirit say to me, "If you go in, you will never find them." I knew that I had just been prayed over by angels and I believe it was because of my obedience to the Holy Spirit.

As I drove home, I realized that I was not able to remember one word that either of them had prayed over me. Not one word! I do not know the beginning, the end, or the middle. The only part I remember is, "I feel led to pray for you!"

I have prayed numerous times that God would let me know the prayer that was prayed over me. But the Holy Spirit told me, "The prayer was for another time that is yet to come!" So, I wait expectantly.

9. Prophetic Dream Comes to Pass

I have always dreamed dreams but only once did the Lord say, "Write your dream!" and I did. He then said, "Interpret your dream." And I did. In the dream, I saw a closed restaurant with a drive-through window. I climbed through the window and began walking around thc chairs that had just been freshly painted. The smell was very strong, so I walked carefully to avoid getting paint on myself. As I walked toward the larger room, I bent over to pick up the book I saw on the floor. There were fifty to sixty people standing around me as I taught from the book I had found. Many people came forward and accepted Christ as their Savior.

In the dream, there were two sisters Joanie and Lee. Lee looked at me with tears in her eyes and said, "I want what you have," and Joanie said, "So do I." Immediately, I laid hands on them both saying, "Silver and gold have I none, but such as I have, I give to you."[59] Suddenly, the Holy Ghost was all over us and they were both filled with the Holy Ghost. His presence was so strong.

Then, I walked over to the drive-in window and saw a car going in the wrong direction. In the car was a

[59] See Acts 3:6

mother and her child. They appeared to be Hispanic, but I wasn't sure. I hollered out the window at them, "Careful, you're going the wrong way!" Then, they were gone. This was the dream as I wrote it fifteen years ago.

What I discovered in the days, months, and years after this dream was this. The restaurant ended up being my catering business. I converted it into *The House of Prayer, Prophecy, and Healing*. I opened my church to young ministers that used it to build up their own ministries.

Seven other churches have been birthed so far. The mother and daughter came into my feeding mission and she and I became close friends, Fe and Irene Nolan. As far as Lee and Joanie are concerned, they grew in the Lord by leaps and bounds. I had taken them to a local church where they were baptized. Lee died within six months and Joanie died within three years. We never know why God does certain things, but I am thankful that Lee and Joanie were saved. They had had such a terrible life, but they both found peace in the Lord, through the Holy Spirit before their death.

Still Growing from Glory to Glory!

In addition to these incidents and experiences with

the Holy Spirit, my ongoing revelations have truly been phenomenal as I continue to be regenerated by Him. Knowing that He dwells in me always gives me such comfort that is unexplainable. He anoints me for service and empowers me to get the job done. When He tells me to do something, He gives me the power and strength to do it. For example, when I was told, "You are to teach," He anointed my teaching from day one. Teaching has become my love, my passion because this is my "calling."

The Holy Spirit bears witness with my spirit, assuring me that I am the child of God. He comforts me in all that I do, giving me joy and peace while setting me at ease in all that I do. Throughout life, I can go forward with confidence, knowing the Holy Spirit is my organizer, according to Acts 13:2, and that when needed, He will release anointing and power to strengthen me in any situation. He will give me discernment and bring things to my remembrance as I need them. He, himself, will teach me according to Nehemiah 9:20, "Thou gave also thy good spirit to instruct them and withheld not their manna from their mouth, and gave them water for their thirst." The good Spirit has fed my hunger and quenched my thirst with the Word of God. He guides my steps daily. All confusion has vanished from my life as I continue being transformed forever.

I am amazed when I think about the spiritual experiences, the closeness and deepness and the glory of those spiritual encounters that I have known. Jesus is merciful and God's love cannot be fathomed. We can have the closeness and friendship of the Holy Spirit there with us, even in our darkest hours. It was the greatest day of my life when I learned of the Holy Spirit. He changed my life, and He changed my ministry.

It all begins with surrender to the Holy Spirit! If I had not been surrendered when I was sent to the restaurant in Fredericksburg, Virginia, and had I not been obedient, I believe that the angels would never have been led to pray over me. Had I not been surrendered and obedient, and tuned into the voice, the unction, the presence of the Holy Spirit, my wonderful daughter would have burned to death in that car on the way back from West Virginia. She would never have married or had four beautiful children and two grandchildren, making me a four-time grandmother and a three-time great grandmother!

In these pages, I have given only a few examples of real life living with the Holy Spirit in my daily life. The things He has done for me, He can also do for you, and even greater things! God is creating a hunger and thirst in each of us that longs to be filled to overflowing with the Holy Spirit, a power an unction or anointing that cannot quinch that thirst. We are longing for Him, His glorious presence. It is a personal baptism in his river that never shall run dry.

Do you know the glorious strengthening power of the Holy Spirit? The Apostle Paul did. In fact, we cannot be strong except in the power of the Holy Spirit. Even Jesus knew Him that way! That's why Jesus promised, "Ye shall receive power after the Holy Ghost comes upon you."[60] What power? The same power that had been manifest in Jesus' and Paul's ministries and in their daily lives can be in your daily life with the Holy Spirit!

There are not enough words in the dictionary to thank you, Lord, for how far you have brought me! I thank the Holy Spirit for purging the sin from my body as He entered my body in the whirlwind through my eyes! I thank the Lord for bringing me peace from the death of my baby and showing me how to forgive my husband. I pray somewhere along the way he met Jesus. Lord, I thank You for the evangelist that took my husband and me to the revival where I walked the aisle to surrender my heart to Jesus. (The strange thing was that the evangelist at one time was the town drunk, who had DT's so bad they committed him to the mental ward of the hospital. When he dried out,

---

[60] See Acts 1:8

he went to AA where he became clean, became a minister, led me to the Lord by taking me to the revival, and the Lord used him mightily in so many lives. This is a good reminder that it is important to never look down on anyone because you never know where they came from or where they are going. You also never know when you might be entertaining angels.)

Holy Spirit, I pray You will never leave me and You will continue to use me and to work through me. I will surrender daily to You and will always be obedient to Your voice. Hallelujah!

Closing Prayer

Lord I pray, make me an instrument of righteousness unto God.

That in the fullness of time we may become one in Christ, in heart, soul, and spirit for His good pleasure. (Philippians 2:13)

I pray that every Christian in our church will commit to inviting one person each week to attend services at our churches.

I pray that each of us will go out of our way to speak to someone in our church we do not know.

I pray someone in your church will start a new Bible Study. I pray we speak to neighbors in our community and invite them to a Bible study, and if you don't have a bible Study, start one. Let us draw closer to Him, and learn to walk out into the deep. Let us climb up Jacob's ladder.

I pray that the Five-Fold ministry will be welcomed back into the churches in every city in this nation and begins the revival that is so deeply needed in this land.

I pray we will grow from glory, to glory, to glory! For I know God works in us to accomplish His purpose.

Let us go to homeless shelters and minister to the lost.

I pray that you will bring each one of us into the authority we have in the name of Jesus. Luke 9:1: Then He called His twelve together and gave them power and authority over all devils and to cure diseases.

Let us repeat that: He [Jesus], called His twelve together [the disciples], and gave them power and authority [we have the power that Jesus had when he was on this earth, and the authority to use the name of Jesus] over all devils, and to cure diseases. We have this authority and power! We know we have this authority, so, let us step out in faith and use what God has given us!

Lord, we long to enter into Heaven at the Rapture of your Church, when you beckon your children Home. For the trumpet will sound, and the dead in Christ shall rise first, and we will meet You in the air, as we enter and will be with You forever.

And Father, we thank You!

About the Author

Sheila Kay is the founder and director of Restoring the Broken Vessel Ministries. Through outreach, teaching, and evangelizing, she teaches from God's Word for today's woman. Sheila is available for Conferences, Seminars, Retreats, and Women's groups, giving testimony of the miracles, signs, and wonders God has bestowed upon her through the wonderful Holy Spirit.

About Manifest Publications

Manifest Publications is the publishing division of Manifest International, LLC. Our objective is to help like-minded ministries and writers produce and distribute materials which proclaim Jesus Christ to all the world and equip the global Church for unity and maturity.

www.manifestinternational.com

www.ingramcontent.com/pod-product-compliance
Lightning Source LLC
LaVergne TN
LVHW010105110826
845155LV00028B/486